REFLECTIONS

LOOKING BACK ON ALL THAT THE LORD HAS BROUGHT ME THROUGH

Sonia Lennon-Passard

ISBN 978-1-68517-024-0 (paperback)
ISBN 978-1-68517-025-7 (digital)

Christian Faith Publishing, Inc.
832 Park Avenue
Meadville, PA 16335
www.christianfaithpublishing.com

All scriptures, unless otherwise stated, are taken from the King James Version of the Holy Bible.

Printed in the United States of America

Contents

Acknowledgments

To my parents, Louise and Aston Lennon, who did the best they could to raise me, I love you both very much!

To my husband, Leslie, a.k.a. Ritchie; my children, Lesley-Ann, Lauren, and Anthony; and my grandsons, Zachary and Nathaniel; I love you all very much.

Thank you for putting up with me and supporting me!

Introduction

This book came about from an encounter I had with a young woman at my church. I was serving at the information desk one evening, and this young woman was also serving there on behalf of a visiting evangelist. We got to talking and among other things. I told her about some of my life experiences. Her reaction was, "You should go on speaking engagements." I told her that I don't do well speaking in front of people but that I am okay speaking one-to-one. Then she said, "Well, you should write a book." A couple weeks later, I bought a book that one of my church sisters wrote and brought it home. My husband commented, "When are you going to write a book?" So here we are!

Chapter 1

The Early Years

I was born on June 7, 1952, to Louise Francis-Williams and Aston Lennon, in Point Hill, Saint Catherine, Jamaica, West Indies. I am the second of three girls. My youngest sister, Fay Veronica, is deceased. She was five years old and died from complications of chicken pox.

My sisters and I are miracles. My mother was told by doctors that she couldn't have children. She was thirty-seven years old and my father was forty-two when I was born. My older sister's name is Cynthia, a.k.a. Miss Joe. She was named after my grandfather Joseph, who died the year when she was born. My younger sister's name is Fay, a.k.a. Whilhel, named after my grandmother Whilhelmina, who died the year when she was born. When I was a teenager, I asked my mother why I did not have another name, and her reply was, "No one in the family died the year that you were born."

My father worked with the public works department. He worked on a truck that went all over Saint Catherine, Jamaica, building roads. I guess he was a construction worker. My mother had a small grocery store, and later she operated a cafeteria in a textile factory. My parents worked very hard to raise us and to make sure we had all we needed. My mother was very strict, and she did not "spare the rod." My father was always jumping in between my mother and us, sometimes getting some of the spanking. I got my last spanking when I was eighteen years old and in front of my new boyfriend, who is now my husband. I ran away and went to my friend's house, but her mother said that I needed to return home. I then went to my father's house, but he told me the same thing. I decided to return home and had a good talk with my mother. We resolved the issue, and the spankings stopped.

My parents separated when I was in high school. My father used to be away working most of the week and would come home on the weekend and some weekdays. One weekend, he told us that he would not be coming back, that he would be living on his own. He said that he and our mother were not getting along. My sister and I were very sad and heartbroken. Sometimes I was ashamed that my parents were not together. They never divorced, and they remained friends.

In 1992, I went to Jamaica to relocate my father; he was now eighty-two years old. I experienced a series of setbacks and disappointments, and my plan was just not working. My mother, realizing what was going on, suggested that I let my father stay at her house. It was a blessing from the Lord. Later that same year, my mother passed away, and my father continued to live there with a family member taking care of him. He passed away in 1999.

My brother Mark came to live with us when he was three months old; I was fourteen. Oh, how we loved him, and oh, how he was spoiled. He was an easy baby to take care of. He did not cry a lot and loved to smile. When he was three, my mother bought him a tricycle, and he would ride on the sidewalk for hours, making peep-peep and vroom-vroom sounds. He was very active, adventurous, loving, and liked to eat. He had such an active imagination. He would play for hours by himself, making things up as he went along. When he was five years old, he pushed a stone up his nostril. We took him to the emergency room, but the doctor could not remove it, so he referred us to the ear, nose, and throat specialist. We had an appointment the next day. A friend of the family visited us that evening and suggested that we let him smell some black pepper. It worked! As soon as he smelled the black pepper, he sneezed, and the stone flew out. We were so relieved. Growing up, he had a dog named Mutt.

They went to the ballpark, the river, basically everywhere together. His closest friends were my husband's two younger brothers, Danny and Chubby. They were six and three years old respectively, and my brother was three when they all met.

As far as I can remember, it was never just my sister, my brother, and I. There were always other children living with us. Before we knew about fostering children, my mother was the original foster mother. My cousin Garth came to live with us so he could attend high school and ended up staying with us after he graduated. He is considered my brother. At one point in my growing up, there were three sisters living with us among other children at various times. Most of these children came to live with us so they could attend school. I remember my mother's aunt came to live with us after she suffered a stroke, and after she passed away, her husband came to stay with us. So many more people have stayed at our house from time to time, for different reasons.

My sister was a vice principal at a boarding school, and on occasion, Orton, a student, would come home to spend the weekend with us. This particular student came to live with us after he graduated high school. Now he is a wonderful, loving brother.

I had a wonderful childhood. Growing up, we did not have phones, tablets, computers, etc. We read books, played games, and played outside a lot. I had to walk about three miles to school one-way. When I was in high school, my mother bought a television set. We were the first on our street to own a television, and a lot of children would come to our house to watch TV, sitting on the living room floor. I loved to climb fruit trees and stayed up on the limb eating fruit. Life was good! My best friend growing up was Sonia, a.k.a. Pam. We have been friends since I was ten, and she was eleven. Now we are like sisters.

I had what I like to call "the second-child syndrome." When my sister and I were growing up, every Easter and Christmas, my mother bought us identical dresses and shoes. When my sister outgrew her dress and shoes, then I got them. I had to wear the same dress and shoes twice, until one day, the hand-me-down shoes would not fit;

they were too small. My feet were bigger than my sister's. Oh, happy day! I had to get my own shoes!

> For thou hast possessed my reins: thou hast covered me in my mother's womb. I will praise thee; for I am fearfully and wonderfully made: marvellous are thy works; and that my soul knoweth right well. (Psalm 139:13–14)

> For we are His workmanship, created in Christ Jesus unto good works, which God hath before ordained that we should walk in them. (Ephesians 2:10)

My parents Louise and Aston Lennon

Chapter 2

BOY MEETS GIRL

In 1969, my mother bought a house in Twickenham Park, Saint Catherine, Jamaica, in a new development. It was a two-bedroom, one-bathroom house with a front porch. It had a spacious front yard with a nice backyard, and we had neighbors all around. We loved it!

Later that year, a family moved in the house exactly across the street from our house. It was the Passard family! Our mothers met and became friends. I found out from taking the bus to school that their son attended my high school. This is how I met my husband. I did not like him at first. I thought he was a show-off. He used to be on his front porch doing handstands, etc. We were seventeen years old and in our senior year. We used to stand at the gate talking, until my mother objected and suggested that we talk on the front porch. We were getting ready for final exams, so then he was allowed into the living room, where we would study. We continued to study together after school. One night, when he was leaving to go to his house, I walked him to the front door, and he kissed me good night. It was then that our relationship as boyfriend and girlfriend started.

We graduated from St. Jago High School in 1970. The school is located in Spanish Town, Saint Catherine, Jamaica. It was founded in 1744 and is one of the oldest continuously operated schools in the Western hemisphere. It is renowned for graduating some of Jamaica's senior military officers, world-class cricketers, academic scholars, performing artists, and Olympic athletes. Its motto is *Labor omnia vincit* (work conquers all, labor conquers all). Ritchie, so he is called by his family, enrolled in the police academy, and I went to work at a government office in Kingston. The police academy was in Port Royal, which is a village at the mouth of Kingston Harbour. It was founded in 1494 by the Spanish and was once the largest city in the Caribbean. It was destroyed by an earthquake and tsunami on June 7, 1692. Now it is a tourist attraction and is being developed as a cruise-ship destination. One of the main attractions is the Giddy House. It was built in 1880 and was originally a royal artillery house meant to store weapons and gunpowder. After Port Royal experienced an earthquake in 1907, the Giddy House partially sank. In 1972, I went to nursing school, University Hospital of the West Indies in Kingston, Jamaica. I stayed on campus. We were nineteen years old. We continued our relationship.

Ritchie graduated from the police academy and was stationed in a crime-ridden area of Kingston, and that made me worry about him a lot. I graduated from nursing school on October 1975 and went to work at the Spanish Town Hospital in my hometown. We continued seeing each other.

Toward the end of 1976, I found out that I was pregnant. We talked it over and decided to get married. Our parents were very supportive. I think they knew we were going to get married at some point. We went to marriage counseling with the Anglican priest and got married on December 3, 1976, at the St. Jago Cathedral in Spanish Town. It was a small wedding on a Friday morning. It was a beautiful morning, and I was on time! We were both happy but nervous. Our parents had a reception for us on Saturday evening, December 4. My husband's mother made and decorated the cake; his grandmother made roti; his father made the curried goat, a traditional Jamaican dish; and my mother and both sides of the family came together and cooked. It was a small and beautiful reception with just family and friends, and the food was so good!

Therefore shall a man leave his father and his mother, and shall cleave unto his wife: and they shall be one flesh. (Genesis 2:24)

Giddy House

Chapter 3

BEING A NURSE

I knew that I wanted to be a nurse since I was a little girl.

As far as I can remember, I wanted to be a nurse, even though I had no knowledge of who a nurse was or what she actually did. When I turned eighteen and graduated from high school, I applied for a program to go to England to study nursing. This was an arrangement with the Jamaican and British governments, where young women could go to England to study nursing. At the end of the program, the nurse would return to Jamaica to work under a contract for three years.

All the arrangements were going well; I got my passport and my smallpox vaccine, which was required at that time. During my physical exam, protein and blood were found in my urine. I was sent to a doctor at the Spanish Town Hospital, my hometown, and was admitted for six weeks for treatment and tests. I was diagnosed with glomerulonephritis, which is the inflammation of the tiny filters in the kidneys.

During the six weeks while I was in the hospital, I had antibiotic treatments, twenty-four-hour urine collections, numerous blood work, and also a kidney biopsy. I was not feeling ill, and the nurses found out that I was trying to pursue a course in nursing. They taught me almost all the practical aspects of nursing. They called me Nursie and gave me a nurse's cap. They sent me on errands to the lab, etc. This experience just reinforced my desire to become a nurse. I did not get to go to England but was accepted to the University Hospital of the West Indies School of Nursing in Kingston, Jamaica.

In 1948, the University College of the West Indies was established in Jamaica at Mona, starting with a faculty of medicine. It was affiliated to the University of London. The University College Hospital was started in November 1948 as a teaching hospital. This was the first teaching hospital in the British West Indies and was based on British teaching hospitals. When I started nursing school, only female students were admitted, the minimum age of entry was eighteen years, and only unmarried students were accepted for training. The majority of students were Jamaicans, but we had three students from other Caribbean islands, one from Belize, one from Trinidad and Tobago, and the third from Guyana.

I remember leaving home to go to nursing school. It was my first time leaving home. I was nineteen years old. I was sad but excited. My boyfriend, now my husband, and his uncle accompanied me. I checked in at the student nurses' residence. My roommate was Karlene, a very nice girl from Falmouth, a town on the north side of Jamaica. We got on very well. Nursing school was hard, but good, and I knew that was what I wanted to do. We started out with a three-month PTS (preliminary training school) program. It consisted of classroom lectures, learning activities, and orientation to the wards. In order to proceed to the rest of the program, we had to pass an examination at the end. Our uniform was candy stripe with a white apron and a nurse's hat and white nurse's shoes. We stayed on campus and ate at the hospital cafeteria. When we were on the night shift, 7:00 p.m. to 7:00 a.m., we would eat breakfast at 6:00 p.m. then go on duty. At about midnight, we would go to lunch. We came off duty at 7:00 a.m., and we would eat supper then go to bed. A lot of good memories! Our batch, as we were called, started out with fifty-two students, and we were batch 70.

When I was in my second year of nursing school, I was twenty years old and working on the orthopedic ward. There was a male patient who had multiple fractures and casts who could not wash himself. I went to give him a bed bath. I had all my equipment on a cart, a textbook set up. I proceeded to give him a bath, and I was going by the book. I finished doing his upper body, covered him up, and turned around to soap the washcloth, when I heard him muttering something. When I turned around, oh my, an erection! I froze. I did not know what to do. In that moment, I decided to pretend that I did not see it. I washed around it and finished that bed bath in record time. It was later that I found out that this was a regular occurrence. That was my most embarrassing moment in nursing school. Needless to say, he started to get washed by the male orderly.

On a more pleasant note, one of my fond memories was a group of us going to a Chinese restaurant in the town. During our nursing program, we were given an allowance. I think it was every two weeks. We would go to this Chinese restaurant, and we each would order something different, then we would put the dishes in the middle of the table, and we would all share. We had a good time, and the food was so delicious! We would then walk back to campus. I made a lot of friends in nursing school, and I remain friends with some of them to this day.

I graduated as a registered nurse in October 1975 and went to work at the Spanish Town Hospital in my hometown. I returned to the University Hospital of the West Indies School of Midwifery and graduated as a midwife in 1981.

I strongly believe that nursing is my passion and that it is a call from God on my life. When I was ready to go off to school, a family member tried to discourage me. He wanted me to be a pharmacist, but thank God for my mother, who said, "Sonia, be whatever you want to be." I have worked as a registered nurse from October 1975 until June 2017, when I retired. I have worked in Jamaica, New York, and Florida, mainly in obstetrics. I have also worked in medical-surgical, pediatrics, and adult ICU. I thank God for the opportunity to serve Him in this capacity.

> "For I know the plans I have for you," declares the Lord, "plans to prosper you and not to harm you, plans to give you hope and a future." (Jeremiah 29:11 NIV)

My student nurse picture

Chapter 4

THE LORD, MY HEALER

In 1977, I was twenty weeks pregnant and was working the 3:00 p.m. to 11:00 p.m. shift at the hospital. I was working at the medical-surgical unit. The routine was that I would get home from work, and while I was in the shower, my husband would be heating up my dinner. I had just finished showering, and while I was drying off, I felt something bulging out between my thighs. I threw the towel away and screamed. My husband and mother came running in. I was brought to the hospital where I worked. On examination, my cervix was completely dilated, and "the bag of water" was bulging out. The doctor was surprised when I said that I was not having any pain. Unfortunately, I had a miscarriage. My daughter was born with a heartbeat, her eyes were fused, and she was gasping a little and tried to open her mouth. Her heartbeat stopped after a couple of minutes, and I just held her. It was so devastating! A very difficult period of our lives. My husband, family, medical staff, and nursing staff were very supportive.

I was diagnosed with an incompetent cervix and was told that for future pregnancies, I had to have a suture placed into my cervix at about twelve weeks of pregnancy to keep it from opening. I was discharged to go home after forty-eight hours.

About one week after, I was discharged from the hospital; I was home resting. My husband had left for work. We were still grieving about the loss of our baby daughter and trying to cope. I noticed that

I began to have real heavy vaginal bleeding. My sister brought me to the emergency room. They started an intravenous infusion, did some blood work, and I was admitted. The obstetrician came to see me, and while he was talking to me, I threw up and passed out.

I found myself walking in this huge field. The grass was very green and beautiful, and there were the most beautiful flowers along the edges of the field. I could hear the most beautiful singing I had ever heard, like a choir, but I did not see anyone. There was a one-room building in the middle of the field with a door that was slightly open. The room had no windows, and it was dark inside. I started to walk toward the door. I put one foot inside, then I heard a voice behind me saying, "Sonia, come back." I came to and realized that it was the obstetrician who was saying, "Sonia, come back." I was told that I went into respiratory arrest. I looked up, and blood was infusing.

I was rushed to the operating room to try to stop the bleeding. My sister stayed with me, and my mother came to the hospital when she heard. The doctor was considering that he might have to do a hysterectomy. My husband was at work on the road, and those days, we did not have cell phones, so he got to the hospital as soon as he heard. I thank God that the doctor got the bleeding under control and did not have to do a hysterectomy. I went on to recover and was discharged. It was a very difficult time in our lives. I was not a believer as yet even though I went to church. One of the nurses gave me a Bible and ministered to me.

Praise be to my God and King! I have two daughters. Lesley-Ann was born in Jamaica, and Lauren was born in New York. I had to have a suture put into my cervix for both pregnancies. I give my Father Lord thanks and praise for my two daughters!

> O give thanks unto the Lord for He is good;
> and His mercy endureth forever. (1 Chronicles
> 16:34)

In June of 1992, my mother passed away in Jamaica. She was in the hospital with congestive heart failure three weeks before. My sister and I flew to Jamaica to be with her. She was discharged; we took her home, spent a few days with her then headed back to our respective homes. Two weeks later, my mother went for her follow-up visit at the doctor, walked into his office, and died in the waiting room from a massive heart attack. I had just gotten to work when I received the news. It was devastating! I went home, made and received some calls, and made arrangements to go to Jamaica.

That night, I did not sleep, and I did not feel like eating. The next day, my friend Shearon picked me up and took me shopping for some things for my trip. I left for Jamaica with my two daughters; they were thirteen and five at the time. My husband was to follow us in a few days. The trip was uneventful. I was picked up at the airport and got to my mother's house. Everyone was helpful and supportive. My friend Pam had already started to take care of some of the funeral arrangements. I was still having a hard time sleeping, and I was not eating; I was only drinking.

The next day, I woke up early, took a shower, and felt cold and shivery, as if I had a fever. My sister, some family members, and I went to the funeral home to continue with the arrangements. I was sitting by my sister in the office when I started to feel really ill. I told her I was not feeling well, and she took me outside to get some fresh air. The next thing I know, I was lying on a lounge chair in the office; I had passed out. I was taken to the doctor's office. My temperature was 105 degrees. I was diagnosed with the flu and was sent home with medication and instructed to rest and drink a lot of fluids.

The next day, I started to vomit. A doctor did a house call and prescribed my medication in liquid form. My father stayed by my bedside the whole time, and I remember my father-in-law made me chicken soup and fed me. I was told that some nurses, former colleagues from the hospital, came to visit and gave me a sponge bath that evening. I have no recollection of that evening and night, until early in the morning, I woke up with the worst headache and could not move my neck. I told my sister that I have meningitis. They took me to the emergency room at the hospital where I used to work. I was admitted, had a spinal tap, diagnosed with viral meningitis, and started on intravenous triple antibiotics and steroids.

I remained in the hospital for ten days on bed rest. My husband flew to Jamaica as soon as he heard about my illness and was a tower of strength to me. It was amazing the amount of care and support shown to me. They had to restrict my visitors. One of my colleagues and friend, Ann-Marie, flew down to Jamaica to be with me. While I was in the hospital, my mother's funeral was taking place. Thank God, I was allowed to go to the church in a wheelchair, but was not allowed to go to the cemetery; also a doctor had to accompany me. It was important to me that I saw my mother one last time. The funeral was so sad. There were so many people there, so much love and support. My brother Mark broke down and cried so hard, his wife had to take him outside.

I was discharged after ten days and went to my mother's house. Three women from the community came to pray for me. I was lying in bed in my sister's room; my father was at my bedside. As they prayed, I felt like a fire started at the top of my head, moved through my body, and came out at the sole of my right foot. One of the women said, "You know you are healed," and I said, "Yes." I got out of bed and started walking around the room hands raised, praising the Lord.

The next day, we flew back to Florida: my husband, my two daughters, my cousin, and a friend. I was seen and examined by my doctor in the emergency room. I was weighing one hundred pounds. The doctor said I was over the meningitis, and I was sent home to recuperate. It was such a difficult time of my life. All the glory belongs to the Lord, I made it through. Thanks to my husband, my daughters, my family, and friends for their support.

But He was wounded for our transgressions, He was bruised for our iniquities: the chastisement of our peace was upon Him: and with His stripes we are healed. (Isaiah 53:5)

Chapter 5

THE BAPTISM

I n 1983, my friend Lillian invited me to her church. We were in the same class in high school. I took my daughter with me; she was four years old. It was a Sunday-night service, and they had a visiting evangelist speaking. The church was full, and the singing was really good. I was not used to that kind of service with clapping and dancing. My mother was Roman Catholic, so we went to church with her, then when I met my husband, I started going to church with him. He was an altar boy in the Anglican Church.

My daughter and I were sitting toward the back of the church. I was listening to the preacher, and suddenly I started to cry. My daughter looked at me and said, "Mommy, why are you crying?" and I said, "I don't know." I tried to stop crying, but I couldn't. When the preacher gave the invitation for salvation, I took my daughter's hand and went to the altar, tears running down my face, and I gave my life to the Lord. I remember that I did not want to go to the altar, but it was like I was drawn there. About ten people prayed the prayer of salvation that night.

I started to read my Bible more. Prior to that, I would only read it when I went to church, but now I was reading it at home. I was determined to serve the Lord and to live a life pleasing to Him.

I continued to go to church and to Bible study. I decided to get baptized and started to go to baptismal classes. My friend was right by my side guiding me. In February 1984, I was baptized. It was a Sunday night, the church was full, and the pool was behind the stage. Each baptismal candidate had to give a testimony before they were baptized. We all had to dress in white and bring our change of clothes. The baptism was done during praise and worship, then we changed and rejoined the service. They baptized the men first and then the ladies. My mother, two of her friends from the community, and my daughter came. My friend was right there by my side assisting me. It was a *glorious* night.

> John answered, saying unto them all, "I indeed baptize you with water; but one mightier than I cometh, the latchet of whose shoes I am not worthy to unloose: He shall baptize you with The Holy Ghost and with fire." (Luke 3:16)

My friend Lillian has since gone to be with the Lord.

Chapter 6

MOVED TO THE UNITED
STATES OF AMERICA

In 1983, I saw an advertisement in the Jamaican newspaper the *Daily Gleaner* that a hospital in Bronx, New York, was recruiting nurses. I went to the interview in Kingston, along with other registered nurses. My husband accompanied me. It was a sunny day as usual in Jamaica. The interview was informal and was held at one of the local hotels. We were told about the hospital, the town, and housing, among other things. One of the interviewers was a nurse manager from the hospital. I found out that she was from my hometown. I knew her family and went to high school with her nieces and nephews. It was a hard decision for me to make; my daughter was only four years old. I discussed my leaving with my husband and family then decided to go when I was informed that the recruiting agency would arrange that my family would be able to go with me.

At the interview, we were shown pictures of furnished apartments that we could rent when we got there, and we were told we would get an advance on our salary. I met a young woman, Claudette, at the interview. We became friends and decided to travel together. On Wednesday, February 29, 1984, we flew from Jamaica to John F. Kennedy International Airport in New York via Air Jamaica airlines. This was the first time I was traveling to a cold country. My mother traveled to New York in the 1970s in the wintertime and told me how cold it was, but I could only imagine. When I stepped out of John F. Kennedy International Airport, I will never forget the experience. Even though I was dressed properly, it was so cold, my nose started to run, my eyes started to water, and my ears felt like they were burning. It was my first time experiencing snow, and I was not happy.

My sister-in-law, Janet, was there to meet us, and two nurse managers picked us up and drove us to the Bronx. It was at night, but I was trying to see everything. There were a lot of high-rise buildings. I was impressed with the fact that the roads were so wide and smooth. On our way, we found out that our apartments were not ready. The hospital put my friend up with a Jamaican nurse and put me up with another Jamaican nurse whom we had not met before. The nurse, Norma, whom I stayed with was very nice; she treated me like family. She lived in a one-bedroom apartment, and she actually gave me the bedroom and slept on the sofa even though I protested. She also let me use her phone to call home so my family would know that I got there safely. I was crying a lot during the night. I missed my family and was in an unexpected situation. I was thankful that my family did not travel with me at that time because it would have been so much more difficult. My daughter was asthmatic then, so my husband and I decided that they would travel to New York in May, when it was warmer. Norma and I are friends to this day.

The next morning, Thursday, my friend and I took the bus to the social security office and then another bus to the hospital. It was so cold! We filled out our paperwork and did our physical exam. We were taken on a tour of the hospital, and everyone we met were very nice. On Monday, we started orientation. It was such a culture shock! Nursing practices were so different from what I was used to. On my first day, a patient accused me of coming to America and taking away the jobs from the Americans. HIV/AIDS was a new thing, and it was my first time taking care of a patient with AIDS. The staff was very supportive during my orientation and transitioning.

On Tuesday, we were told that our apartment was ready. My friend and I decided to share an apartment until our family arrived in order to save money. We went to apartment 16G in the hospital residence, and the apartment manager opened the door. We were shocked. There was only a refrigerator and a stove in the apartment. All we had was our clothes and shoes and our personal items. We were told that there were no furnished apartments in the building. On inquiring where we would sleep, the housing manager went by the hospital and brought us two storm cots. I was crying, and I was ready to return home. We also did not receive the advance on our salary as promised. I called my sister-in-law, Janet, God bless her, and she came and brought us everything that we would need to help us during this difficult transition. She brought us a twin bed, a television, plates, cups, forks, sheets, blankets, pillows, etc., and then she took us to the grocery store to get some food. Praise God for my sister-in-law, who has since gone to be with the Lord. I will never forget her kindness. My friend and I finished our orientation, and we started working on the medical-surgical floor. I worked the 7:00 a.m. to 3:00 p.m. shift, and she worked the 3:00 p.m. to 11:00 p.m. shift.

My husband and daughter joined me in New York in May 1984. My friend moved into her own apartment, and I was now able to buy a few pieces of furniture. When I went to pick them up at the airport, I was worried that my daughter would not remember me, which looking back was kind of silly. When the door opened at the terminal, she came running, shouting, "Mummy! Mummy!" Guess what, more crying. I stayed three years in New York, had my second daughter in 1986, then migrated to sunny Florida in July 1987 and worked at a local hospital until I retired in June 2017.

I am writing this in 2021. God has been so good to me. I am living in Florida with my husband, close to my children, my son-in-law, and my grandsons.

> Let your conversation be without covetousness: and be content with such things as ye have: for He hath said: I will never leave thee nor forsake thee. (Hebrews 13:5)

> But my God shall supply all your need according to His riches in glory by Christ Jesus. (Philippians 4:19)

Chapter 7

LOOKING FOR A CHURCH

When we moved to New York, my daughter attended a day care at the Baptist church around the corner from the apartment building where we lived. It was very convenient for drop-off and pickup. The workers at the day care were nice and caring. The church was an all-black church. We decided to start attending that church mainly because it was convenient and in walking distance from where we lived. My second daughter was christened there in 1986.

In 1987, we moved to Florida, and we started to look for a church. The children and I started to go to the church connected to the day care that my second daughter was attending. This church was an all-black church. The first time we attended, I was looking around and did not see another person of a different color. I was not comfortable with that. I always said that I wanted to go to a "mixed church" because that's what heaven is going to look like. We continued to attend that church until we bought a house in 1988 and moved from that area. My coworker invited me to her church that was close to where I lived. I attended the church on Sunday morning, and unlike the other church, it was an all-white church. I was looking around and did not see another person of a different color. We attended that church until 1989 when another coworker, Gloriana, invited me to her church. The Sunday morning I attended, I knew that this was my church. The greeters at the door were so friendly, praise and worship was so good, and the preacher preached the Word of God. The congregation was mixed. We continued going to that church. I became a greeter, and my children were involved in children's ministry.

The pastor started to teach on the Holy Spirit and said that after a few weeks, he was going to pray for people who wanted to be filled with the Holy Spirit, with the evidence of speaking in tongues. During a Sunday-evening service, he called people up, and about thirty people went to the altar. We stood in a line across the front of the church. My friend was standing beside me; she is the one who invited me to the church. The pastor started at one end of the line and worked his way down. I was excited and praising the Lord and repeating, "I love you." The pastor came by me and said, "Do you love Him?" and I said, "Yes." Then the pastor said, "Well, stop speaking English," and immediately I heard some strange sounds coming out of my mouth. Twenty-one people got filled with the Holy Spirit that night.

The children and I continued to go to that church. My husband joined us in 2006. I retired in 2017 and moved to Jacksonville. I was told by the then pastor of the church about a church in Jacksonville. My husband and I visited, and we loved it. The congregation was mixed. We love the pastor, his wife, and his daughter, and it feels like home. At my former church, they had gotten new chairs and donated the old chairs to other churches. It so happened that my new church was one of the churches that received some of the old chairs. My husband and I are sitting on the same chairs twice. *Hallelujah!*

Chapter 8

HOW THE LORD
HAS USED ME

In the year 2000, I needed some extra money for a project and was thinking about working some extra hours to cover the expenses. I decided I did not want to work extra at my current job, so I started to look around at other places. It is surprising how the Lord speaks to us in the most unusual places. One day, I was sitting on the toilet when the Holy Spirit said to me, "Why don't you go over to the jail to work?" I was like, the jail! That cannot be the Lord. I had worked in the hospital for all of my nursing career and had never set foot in a jail. I dismissed it, but it still kept coming in my mind. I have a friend who used to work at the jail, so I called her, and we talked about her experience working there, and I got to ask questions. One night, while I was at work, we had a patient who was under police guard, and I spoke to the deputy regarding her working at the jail. She actually discouraged me.

I was still undecided. One night, one of my coworkers gave me an advertisement that she had cut out of the newspaper about nursing jobs at the jail. She heard me talking about it. I called the number, went in for an interview and a medication test, and was hired on the spot. I was sent for security clearance and got my employee badge. I started to work per diem on the night shift. I was a little nervous at first but quickly adjusted. I was working there for approximately six months and was working on the female section one night when the clanging of the doors got my attention. The deputies were bringing in some new inmates. I looked up and saw one of my friends being brought in. When she saw me, she started to cry and told me all that led up to her arrest. It was a sad night!

In the morning, when I got ready to leave, she asked me to call her lawyer, which I did. She got out of the jail that day. A couple days later, I went to see her, and we talked. She told me that the Lord sent me over the jail that night and that I had saved her life. It was then that I realized why I was sent to the jail to work.

> "For my thoughts are not your thoughts,
> neither are your ways my ways," saith the Lord.
> "For as the heavens are higher than the earth,
> so are my ways higher than your ways, and my
> thoughts than your thoughts." (Isaiah 55:8–9)

Chapter 9

THE LORD, MY PROTECTOR

When I was fourteen years old, my cousin picked me up to take me to see my mother at work. His car was really old. On the driver's side, the door was tied shut with a rope, and on the passenger side, the inside lock on the door was broken, so you had to put your hand outside to open it. We were driving along and talking when the passenger door started to rattle. Just then, he was going around a corner, and I fell out of the car in the middle of the road. Cars were coming at me. I heard a lot of braking. My cousin got to me quickly. I was scared, but my only injury was a skinned left hip and thigh. Thank God I was not hit by a car.

On another occasion, one of my ex-coworkers was in town, and a bunch of us decided to go to lunch. I decided to take my second daughter with me; she was probably ten years old. We headed to the restaurant talking all the way. She was sitting in the passenger seat. We had a great time at the restaurant. The food and the get-together was good. We started to head home, and my daughter wanted to sit in the back seat so she could read a book. She sat in the seat behind me. As we were headed home, I was driving on one of the main roads in the right lane. I was passing a strip mall when suddenly a Ford Bronco drove out of the mall and into the passenger side of my car. My car spun around two times in the middle of the road as I was hanging on tight to the steering wheel. I heard a lot of cars braking. I stopped with the car headed in the opposite direction. The driver of the Ford Bronco just drove off and did not even check to see if we were all right. Out of the corner of my eye, I saw him giving us a salute!

I decided to get off the road, so I drove into the strip mall. We were really shaken up, and my daughter was crying. We checked ourselves, and we had no visible injuries and no pain. I held my daughter's hands and prayed and thanked the Lord for protecting us. I then called 911 and my husband. The police and paramedics came. We were both okay and did not need to go to the hospital. The car had to be towed away. The passenger side, especially the front, was all torn up. I thank my Lord to this day that my daughter decided to sit in the back seat behind me on our way home. If she was sitting in the front passenger seat, the outcome would have been so much worse. Thank You, Lord! You protected us that day and every day.

A few years ago, I was alone at home and was cleaning my bathroom. I reached up to clean the tiles and lost my balance. I was about to fall when I felt a huge hand encircle my waist and steadied me.

> For He shall give His angels charge over thee, to keep thee in all thy ways. They shall bear thee up in their hands, lest thou dash thy foot against a stone. (Psalm 91:11–12)

> But the mercy of the Lord is from everlasting to everlasting upon them that fear Him, and His righteousness unto children's children. (Psalm 103:17)

Chapter 10

THE LORD, MY PROVIDER

The first house that my husband and I bought together, in 1988, was an older house built in 1969. We loved that house mainly because it was our first house. We were living there for about five years when I noticed a water spot in the family-room ceiling. I pointed it out to my husband when he came home from work. We talked it over and decided that we were going to put a new roof on the house. There was a roofer at the church I was attending at the time, so I decided to call the office for an estimate. The receptionist was very pleasant but told me that the roofing company does not do residential roofs anymore, only commercial roofs.

My husband and I looked in the yellow pages and ended up getting three estimates. One was fifteen thousand dollars, the second was seven thousand, and the third was eight thousand. We decided that I would take the estimates to church with me and ask the roofer what he thought.

The roofer was an usher, and I was a greeter. I didn't know him well; we just greeted each other in passing. I went to church early and met him outside. I told him that I had called his office and what I was told by the receptionist. I showed him the estimates and asked him if he knew any of the companies and whom he thought I should go with. He looked at them, and to my surprise, he said, "I will do your roof for you, and it won't cost you a cent," and he put the estimates in his pocket. Those were his exact words. I was shocked! I just stood there, not saying a word, thinking, *Did I hear him right?* when he repeated himself. I just gave him a big hug!

So one day, about two weeks later, I was home and heard a knock on the door. It was the roofer. He wanted to know what kind of tiles and what color I wanted. I really had no idea, so he pointed to the house across the street and said that would look good, so we agreed. One night about a week later, I was at work, and my daughter called to say that the roofer would be at the house at 7:00 a.m. I got home at about 8:00 a.m., and there were three dump trucks in my yard with about ten men tearing off my roof. My husband had already left for work. I am thinking that I need to go fix them something to eat and get them some water and drinks, etc., but when I offered, they said thanks, but they came prepared with all that stuff.

In that one day, they replaced our roof and replaced all the eaves around the house, even though it was not included in the estimate. They cleaned up the yard; it was spotless. The next day, the roofer came, attached the permit outside the window, and told me that the inspector will come for the inspection. Two days later, the inspector came, said everything was good, and that we could take down the permit. Up to that point, I did not spend a cent!

> Delight thyself also in the Lord; and He shall give thee the desires of thine heart. Commit thy way unto the Lord; trust also in Him; and He shall bring it to pass. (Psalm 37:4–5)

A number of years ago, our dryer was overheating. When we bought the house, both the washer and dryer were old. I tried to use it by turning it off several times during the cycle. It was apparent that we needed a new one. We did not want to use our credit card, so we decided to save for one. In the meanwhile, I went to the laundromat to dry our clothes. Approximately two weeks after we started doing that, I went to the mailbox and saw a letter from my friend who lived in Saudi Arabia. She sent me a check for five hundred dollars. Thank you, Lord! I had done a few favors for her, and she was just showing her appreciation. We could now buy, along with the money we saved, not only a dryer but a new washing machine. The Lord provided for us and all the way from Saudi Arabia!

> But my God shall supply all your need according to His riches in Glory by Christ Jesus. (Philippians 4:19)

Chapter 11

THE LORD, MY COMFORTER

The year 2020 was a difficult one. There was a lot of racial tension, natural disasters, a presidential election and a COVID-19 pandemic. Everything changed. Churches and schools were closed. Nonessential businesses were closed. People were dying from the virus. People lost their jobs. There was a lot of chaos, fear, and frustration.

On the morning of November 17, 2020, my sister-in-law, Judy, called me to say that my brother Mark had passed away. The news was so devastating! My sister-in-law and I were crying and screaming on the phone. I was just about finished writing this book about all that the Lord has brought me through, and once again, He was there to see me through another crisis.

Mark was born on May 3, 1966. Many of those who knew Mark during his childhood remember him as a youngster with an incredible inquiring mind. He was involved in activities from sports to academics to being a cadet, a faithful friend, and a supporting family member. His young brain absorbed just about everything to which he was exposed. He was in many ways an average young man. He was fun, loving, mischievous, and adventurous. Most of all, he was an honorable person.

Mark successfully attended and graduated from St. Jago High School in Spanish Town, Jamaica, where he excelled in all areas of his secondary school life. He also represented Jamaica at the CARIFTA

(Caribbean Free Trade Association) games, where his main discipline was javelin. He obtained an associate's degree in business administration and management and later pursued additional studies with a concentration in management information systems.

One of his favorite hobbies was music, especially being the DJ at family functions, along with taking family photos and videos at any opportunity. He also enjoyed debating current events with family and friends. Let us not endure prolonged sadness as Mark goes on his journey, since we hope to see him again. His faithfulness puts him in the line for a resurrection to perfect life. May his soul rest in peace, and may perpetual light shine upon him. Rest in peace, Mark!

My brother passed away in Connecticut on November 17, and his funeral was on November 27, the day after Thanksgiving. I wanted to go to the funeral but was afraid because of COVID-19. I prayed about it, and twice the Father told me, "You need to go. I will take care of you." I left on Thanksgiving Day still afraid. I flew from Jacksonville to Connecticut, with a layover in Charlotte. I attended the funeral. I flew back the Saturday after Thanksgiving, from Connecticut to Dallas and then to Jacksonville. All four flights were full. All four airports were crowded. I went into self-quarantine on my return and did my COVID-19 test on day 6, which was negative. On day 15, I repeated the test, and it was negative.

I enter God's *presence* with *praise* and *thanksgiving*. I am so thankful to You, my Lord, and I *bless* Your *name*! For You are good, Your mercy is everlasting, and Your truth endures to all generations (Psalm 100:4–5; paraphrased)!

> God is not a man that He should lie; neither the Son of man that He should repent: hath He said and shall He not do it? Or hath He spoken and shall He not make it good? (Numbers 23:19)

> Blessed be God, even the Father of our Lord Jesus Christ, the Father of mercies, and the God of all comfort; Who comforteth us in all our tribulation, that we may be able to comfort

them which are in any trouble, by the comfort wherewith we ourselves are comforted of God. (2 Corinthians 1:3–4)

I give my Abba Lord all the *glory* and the *praise*! All the *hallelujahs* and the *thanks* belongs to Him. My tests came back negative!

Mark Anthony Brown Sr.

Chapter 12

Israel Trip 2012

My husband and I had been thinking for a couple years about taking a trip to Israel. We finally decided to go in 2012. My husband listened to a leading evangelist a lot, so we decided to go with his group. We contacted the network and got all of our papers and passports in order. We made arrangements through a travel agency. We were very excited! A few months before our trip, there was a lot of unrest in Israel and surrounding areas. November 14 to November 21 was the 2012 Israeli operation in the Gaza Strip. Our trip was scheduled for that November. Almost all of our friends and family members were telling us not to go. Our daughters expressed concerns about us going. We were at peace, and we wanted to go. The evangelist flew into Israel ahead of us and would send us daily emails about what was going on. He said it was safe, and we should come. We finalized the arrangements.

In November 2012, Shearon, our friend, dropped us off at the local airport where we would fly to Philadelphia to catch a connecting flight to Israel. We boarded the plane at the local airport. We met two women on the flight who were also going on the tour. The airplane started to taxi for takeoff, and suddenly we heard a real awful noise. A woman in the seat behind us said, "What is that?" The pilot came over the intercom and said that there was something wrong with the hydraulics, and there would be a delay. We were sitting there for maybe an hour, then the pilot announced that we had to return

41

to the gate and make arrangements to get on other flights. When we got to the counter, there was no flight available that we could get on to make our connection in Philadelphia, so we had to return home. Our friend picked us up. We were booked for the next day on a flight to New York and then to Israel. We were very disappointed. One of my family members said that it was a sign that we should not go. We were determined to go and looked forward to the trip the next day.

The next day, Shearon dropped us off at the local airport again. We met our two traveling companions, and we headed off to New York without incident. Our flight to Israel was uneventful. The flight was ten hours nonstop. We left in the evening. The flight attendant gave us a toothbrush-and-toothpaste combination and a blindfold, and they dimmed the lights. We got to Tel Aviv in the afternoon; we were so excited. A young woman from the agency met us and escorted us through customs and outside, where we were picked up in a minivan and brought to the hotel. The check-in was easy; they were expecting us.

The hotel room was beautiful and comfortable, and we were tired, so we had a good night's sleep. The next morning, we had to wake up early, get ready, go down to the lobby to have breakfast, and be on the bus by 6:30 a.m. Breakfast was buffet-style. They served American and local foods. There was something for everyone, and it was delicious. The service was also outstanding. We got on the bus on time. We were so excited. The tour buses were named after colors. We were assigned to the orange bus. Our tour guide was an Israeli who spoke perfect English and told us he used to live in New York and drove taxicabs. He did a head count and discovered that he was three over. We explained that we were a day late. We were welcomed and got our tour backpack and hat. It was so exciting driving and looking at the scenery. We stopped at designated places along the tour, got bathroom breaks, and stopped off for lunch at local restaurants, all included in our trip. All the buses would meet at some of the places, for example, when the evangelist was doing a teaching. We would return to the hotel after the tour, have dinner, buffet-style again, and a lot of delicious food. Everyone basically met for meals, so we got to know some people. We would then head up to our room for a good night's rest for the next day.

We visited a lot of places. These were some of our favorites. Our first favorite: We all sailed out on the sea of Galilee in three boats. The boats were anchored side by side. The evangelist was in the middle boat, and he did a teaching. The sea was calm, and the weather was cool. It was cool while we were there. We wore a sweater or jacket. A few days, it rained a little.

Our next favorite: We got baptized in the river Jordan, the river that Jesus was baptized in. The water was cold! We were instructed to put our arms around each other, and we were baptized together. That was special!

Our next favorite was our visit to Bethlehem. We had to cross the border, and we were told to bring our passport. At the border, our bus driver and tour guide could not cross over, so they had to get off the bus and wait until we returned. We got a new bus driver and tour guide just for Bethlehem. While sitting on the bus at the border, two soldiers with long guns came in through the back door then walked through the bus and exited through the front door. We loved the Bethlehem tour, and we got to do some shopping.

Our next favorite was the Dead Sea tour. The water was like mud. It is believed that mineral extracts from the Dead Sea are natural moisturizers that protect, rejuvenate, and fortify the skin. There were a lot of people there from different countries. People were getting into the sea and smearing mud all over their faces and bodies. They had showers set up on the beach to wash off. There was a group from Africa, and this woman was just out in the open showering topless. Most people were just staring, but we realized that it was her custom. The trip to the tomb that Jesus was thought to be buried in was very special. We got to go inside about two people at a time. We all had Communion outside of the tomb.

On the tours, we saw people from all over the world. We did a lot of walking. Some of the places, for example, the excavation sites, there were no roads to drive on. We also walked the route that Jesus walked to the cross.

On our last day of the tour, we got up early. My husband was not feeling well, and he had a fever. I suggested that we should skip the tour that day so he could get some rest. He insisted on going. We did our usual morning prayer, I gave him some Tylenol, and we went down to breakfast. I was a little worried about him, but he did well.

One of our last stops on the tour was the garden of Gethsemane. We had a digital camera that we were taking pictures with everywhere we went. My husband took a picture of one of the trees in the garden. When he looked at the picture to check if it was okay, there was a sword/cross in the picture. Most people in the group crowded around to take a look. I am glad that he did not let his feeling ill stop him from going on tour that day. Most people gave us their email addresses so we could send the picture to them. We returned to the United States safe and sound, thank God! I believe that every Christian should visit Israel at least once. The Bible comes alive when you are there.

The Garden of Gethsemane Israel 2012

My tabernacle also shall be with them: yea, I will be their God, and they shall be my people. And the heathen shall know that I the Lord do sanctify Israel, when my sanctuary shall be in the midst of them for evermore. (Ezekiel 37:27–28)

Chapter 13

THE SEPARATION

In 2006, my husband and I were in a bad place in our marriage. There was a lot of strife. We were just not getting along. Our daughters were on their own; we were empty nesters. I made the decision to leave my husband. I was not thinking at all of divorcing him, but I just wanted some peace. We put our house on the market, and it sold quickly. I bought a condominium, and my husband bought a house. We split the furniture and the money, and we parted ways. It was very hard being on my own; the first night, I did not sleep at all. I was anxious and afraid. This was the first time in my life that I was living alone.

I got saved and baptized in 1984, and for years, I have been going to church and taking my children with me. My husband and I used to go to church for a few years after we were married, but later, he only attended if the children were in a program. I kept praying for him to be saved for approximately eighteen years. I did everything that people told me to do. For example, a friend in New York told me to lay out his clothes and shoes for church on the bed on Sunday morning, but not to say anything to him. I did this for two Sunday mornings. He ignored them, never said a word, and kept going. I stopped trying and stressing when one of my patients at the hospital told me one night, "You cannot save him. Your job is to pray." So I kept praying!

Two weeks after we separated, my husband called me crying, saying he did not like the way his life was going, and he was sorry for all that we went through. It was a Wednesday night, and he asked me if I was going to church. He wanted to come with me, so I picked him up. He was all dressed up, had on a jacket, and he had bought a new Bible. I told him we usually do not dress up on Wednesday nights, but he did not change.

We got to church, and after we were seated, I went to the pastor's office before the service started and told him that my husband was in church. The pastor said, "It is because of your praying and your faithfulness." I was so excited! During praise and worship, my husband stood up taking part. He was clapping, and to top it off, when the offering plate passed, he put money in it. I was shocked! At the end of service, the pastor gave an altar call for salvation. He did not go up, but I sensed in my spirit that he wanted to. I dropped him off, and he wanted me to pick him up Sunday. I went home.

I had the feeling that he was going to go to the altar on Sunday, so I called his mother and other relatives and invited them to church. It was a beautiful Sunday morning, and the church was full. When the pastor gave the invitation for salvation, I was standing next to him, praying quietly with my eyes closed. I felt when he passed by me. I opened my eyes, and he was on his way to the altar. His mother was rejoicing! I went to the altar with him all the while just crying. After we prayed, I went back to the reception area with him where they meet with new converts. It was a glorious day!

This was February 2006. By May 2006, my husband was attending church regularly, paying his tithes, became a member of the church, and started serving. He is a camera operator to this day.

Praise God!

The baptism

It was a beautiful Sunday evening, and it was at the beach. The sea was quite rough that evening. Twenty-one people got baptized, and family members were in attendance. My husband's mother and our first daughter came with us. We took beach chairs and blankets

47

and sat on the beach while the baptism was taking place. My husband had on shorts and a white polo-neck shirt. It was so awesome when he walked out to the pastor and got baptized!

> John answered, saying unto them all, "I indeed baptize you with water, but one mightier than I cometh, the latchet of whose shoes I am not worthy to unloose: He shall baptize you with the Holy Ghost and with fire." (Luke 3:16)

Chapter 14

WALMART

Walmart has become my favorite store since I retired. This is where we buy our groceries and some other stuff. Recently, my husband gave me a one-hundred-dollar bill for Christmas, and the Lord told me to give it away. I was thinking of whom should I give it to and came up with some names of people who I thought needed it. During my prayer time, the Lord told me to use it to pay for the groceries of the person behind me in the checkout line.

I am in Walmart, I am finished shopping, and I went to the checkout line, but there is no one behind me, which was kind of unusual. What to do! I saw a young woman from my church in the other checkout line. We greeted each other, and I am thinking, it must be for her, but the Lord said, give it to the person behind you. Just then, a young woman with a toddler joined the line. I looked in her cart, thinking if the money was going to be enough, but I obeyed. I finished checking out, then I said to the young woman, "Jesus loves you, and I am going to pay for your groceries." She looked shocked! I told the cashier that I was going to pay for this young woman's groceries, gave her the one-hundred-dollar bill, and she said, "Yes, ma'am," and I left the store.

But my God shall supply all your need
according to His riches in Glory by Christ Jesus.
(Philippians 4:19)

Another day, I am in Walmart, and I saw an elderly gentleman shopping in one of those riding carts. He came up to my husband and I and said in a commanding voice, "Do you know Jesus?" We said yes, then he said, "Are you on your way to heaven?" We said yes, then he rode off and went to the next person and did the same. Later, I saw him in the store and told him that I wanted to be like him, but I did not have the courage and the boldness. He told me to trust God and that this was his ministry.

Wait on the Lord: be of good courage, and
He shall strengthen thine heart: wait I say on the
Lord. (Psalm 27:14)

Chapter 15

SOME OF MY FAVORITE SCRIPTURES

My favorite Psalm is Psalm 91.

1. He that dwelleth in the secret place of the Most High shall abide under the shadow of the Almighty.
2. I will say of the Lord, He is my refuge and my fortress: my God; in Him will I trust.
3. Surely He shall deliver thee from the snare of the fowler, and from the noisome pestilence.
4. He shall cover thee with His feathers, and under His wings shalt thou trust: His truth shall be thy shield and buckler.
5. Thou shalt not be afraid for the terror by night; nor for the arrow that flieth by day;
6. Nor for the pestilence that walketh in darkness; nor for the destruction that wasteth at noonday.
7. A thousand shall fall at thy side, and ten thousand at thy right hand; but it shall not come nigh thee.
8. Only with thine eyes shalt thou behold and see the reward of the wicked.
9. Because thou hast made the Lord, which is my refuge, even the Most High, thy habitation;

10. There shall no evil befall thee, neither shall any plague come nigh thy dwelling.
11. For He shall give His angels charge over thee, to keep thee in all thy ways.
12. They shall bear thee up in their hands, lest thou dash thy foot against a stone.
13. Thou shalt tread upon the lion and adder: the young lion and the dragon shalt thou trample under feet.
14. Because he hath set his love upon me, therefore will I deliver him: I will set him on high, because he hath known my name.
15. He shall call upon me, and I will answer him: I will be with him in trouble; I will deliver him, and honour him.
16. With long life will I satisfy him, and show him my salvation.

Amen!

I am writing this during the COVID-19 pandemic of 2020, and I find this to be a very appropriate Psalm for the times that we are now living in. I believe that we should repeat this daily!

These are some of my favorite verses.

> For thou hast possessed my reins: thou hast covered me in my mother's womb. I will praise thee; for I am fearfully and wonderfully made: marvellous are thy works; and that my soul knoweth right well. (Psalm 139:13–14)

> Nay, in all things we are more than conquerors through Him that loved us. For I am persuaded that neither death, nor life, nor angels, nor principalities, nor powers, nor things present, nor things to come, nor height, nor depth, nor any other creature, shall be able to separate us from the love of God, which is in Christ Jesus our Lord. (Romans 8:37–39)

For the weapons of our warfare are not carnal, but mighty through God to the pulling down of strongholds. Casting down imaginations, and every high thing that exalteth itself against the knowledge of God, and bringing into captivity every thought to the obedience of Christ. (2 Corinthians 10:4–5)

And they said, "Believe on the Lord Jesus Christ, and thou shalt be saved, and thy house." (Acts 16:31)

But He was wounded for our transgressions, He was bruised for our iniquities: the chastisement of our peace was upon Him; and with His stripes we are healed. All we like sheep have gone astray; we have turned everyone to his own way; and the Lord hath laid on Him the iniquity of us all. He was oppressed, and He was afflicted, yet He opened not His mouth: He was brought as a lamb to the slaughter, and as a sheep before her shearers is dumb, so He opened not His mouth. (Isaiah 53:5–7)

The Lord bless thee, and keep thee: The Lord make His face shine upon thee, and be gracious unto thee: The Lord lift up His countenance upon thee, and give thee peace. (Numbers 6:24–26)

For God hath not given us the spirit of fear; but of power, and of love, and of a sound mind. (2 Timothy 1:7)

Ye are of God, little children, and have overcome them: because greater is He that is in you, than he that is in the world. (1 John 4:4)

For we walk by faith, not by sight. (2 Corinthians 5:7)

Therefore I say unto you, what things soever ye desire, when ye pray, believe that ye receive them, and ye shall have them. And when ye stand praying, forgive, if ye have ought against any: that your Father also who is in heaven may forgive you your trespasses. (Mark 11:24–25)

"For my thoughts are not your thoughts, neither are your ways my ways," saith the Lord. "For as the heavens are higher than the earth, so are my ways higher than your ways, and my thoughts higher than your thoughts." (Isaiah 55:8–9)

"No weapon that is formed against thee shall prosper; and every tongue that shall rise against thee in judgement thou shalt condemn. This is the heritage of the servants of the Lord, and their righteousness is of me," saith the Lord. (Isaiah 54:17)

Chapter 16

Daily Declarations

My friend Claudette, of fifty years, who is a licensed minister, sent me these daily declarations, and I would like to share them.

I am *highly favored* of God.
I am valuable, qualified, forgiven, and loved.
I am confident and courageous.
I have extraordinary opportunities given to me.
I attract God-inspired ideas that produce great wealth.
I am enjoying a debt-free life.
I have a prosperous mindset.
I am blessed to be a blessing.
As for me and my house, we will serve the Lord.
I have the grace to embrace every season of life.
I am in the best shape of my life.
I am fit, firm, and muscular.
I enjoy working out.
I have a high metabolism.
I am healthy and full of energy.
I am disciplined, spirit, soul, and body.
I am easily shedding pounds and inches.
I am free from the torment over food.
I have organs and hormones that function properly.

I am my ideal weight.
I eat whatever I want and still maintain my perfect weight.
I have the wisdom of God to make the best decisions.
I live with passion and purpose.
I know that all things are working together for my good.
I am fulfilling my life assignment down to the last detail.
Father, according to Your Word, I declare:

Whatever I ask for in prayer, I believe that I have received it, and it will be mine (Mark 11:24; paraphrased).

My God is able to do exceedingly abundantly above all that I ask or think, according to the power that works in me (Ephesians 3:20; paraphrased).

I call those things that are not as though they already are, and I thank You for it in Jesus's name! Amen (Romans 4:17; paraphrased).